THIRTEEN REASONS WHY NOT
A STEP-BY-STEP GUIDE FOR HELPING DEPRESSED & SUICIDAL TEENAGERS

MATT MIZELL

© Matt Mizell 2017

All rights reserved. Written permission must be secured from the publisher to use or reproduce any part of this book, except for brief quotations in critical reviews or articles.

Published in Carlsbad, California, by Mizell Publishing. Mizell Publishing and the coat of arms logo are protected by copyright.

Available from Amazon.com and other retail outlets.

For more information, email matt@mattmizell.com or visit mattmizell.com.

ISBN-13: 978-1545540169 ISBN-10: 1545540160

Scriptures taken from the Holy Bible, New International Version®, NIV®. Copyright © 1973, 1978, 1984, 2011 by Biblica, Inc.™ Used by permission of Zondervan. All rights reserved worldwide. www.zondervan.com The "NIV" and "New International Version" are trademarks registered in the United States Patent and Trademark Office by Biblica, Inc.™

This book has no affiliation with the Netflix Originals® series or Jay Asher's book titled "Thirteen Reasons Why".

Dedicated to those who courageously serve others in crisis.

"If you're not making someone else's life better, then you're wasting your time. Your life will become better by making other lives better."

— WILL SMITH

CONTENTS

9	Are You Suicidal?
11	Preface
15	STEP #1: Know Your Role
18	STEP #2: Protect Yourself
21	STEP #3: Don't Make Promises You Can't Keep
24	STEP #4: Find a Place to Talk
26	STEP #5: Be Present
29	STEP #6: Listen for Warning Signs
31	STEP #7: Don't Freak Out
33	STEP #8: Keep Asking Questions
38	STEP #9: Reassure Them
40	STEP #10: Give Solid Advice
42	STEP #11: Triage Them
52	STEP #12: Equip Them
54	STEP #13: Follow Up

55   Quick Reference Guide

57   Conclusion

58   Acknowledgements

59   About the Author

ARE YOU SUICIDAL?

If you are someone who is personally struggling with depression or contemplating suicide, this book is not intended for you.

This book is intended to equip others with practical steps for how to help those who are in your situation.

If you have been struggling with anxiety or depression, but are not currently contemplating suicide, turn to page 55 to view helpful resources available in your area.

If you are currently experiencing suicidal thoughts, please stop reading this book and call or text the National Suicide Hotline at (800) 273-8255 for immediate assistance and support.

THIRTEEN REASONS WHY NOT

PREFACE

On March 31, 2017, Netflix released an original series called "Thirteen Reasons Why" that became the most-popular Netflix series ever in just 7 days.

The series, produced by Selena Gomez, is based on a book by the same title written by Jay Asher. Both the series and the book are all about a girl named Hannah who took her own life after a series of students bullied her in high school.

While millions of teenagers watched the series, several faith-based, mental health and news organizations blasted Netflix for seemingly advocating suicide by creating an entertaining drama built around the subject.

Regardless of whether Netflix should or should not have produced the show, the result was that the topic of suicide was quickly catapulted into discussions worldwide due to the viral popularity of the show.

If you have worked with high school students for any

significant length of time, you likely have first-hand experience of dealing with students facing anxiety, depression or suicidal thoughts.

This guide is intended to equip you with practical steps on how to deal with teenagers whom you discover to be struggling with severe anxiety, depression or suicide.

The presumption is that you are not a trained professional or you probably have your own process and previous training for how to deal with such hurting students.

In full disclosure, I am not a licensed or professional counselor either. However, the following 13 steps have been compiled after much research into mental health resources and interviews of professional counselors, therapists, and police officers.

If you have additional questions, please contact a local trained professional in your area. For ideas of whom you may contact, see the Quick Reference Guide on page 55 of this book.

My hope is that this book will equip you with confidence and practical steps so that after a student confides in you of their suicidal thoughts, they will attribute your conversation and subsequent steps as the thirteen reasons why they did *not* choose to take their own life.

THIRTEEN REASONS WHY NOT

STEP #1: KNOW YOUR ROLE

You are a First Responder.

Whether you want this role or not, if a teenager comes to you and confides they are going through depression or are contemplating suicide, you could very well be the first person whom they have told.

Consider it an honor.

While many people may consider this to be a scary place to be, it likely is not something you chose. Whether you would have chosen your role or not, you must respond!

Do not shy away from the responsibility. You have the opportunity to respond, intervene, direct, engage, listen to, and potentially save the student who just confided in you.

This is a serious responsibility.

While it is crucial for you as a First Responder to actually respond, please also understand that your role is not to fix the student.

Their choices are solely their choices. You cannot make all of their choices, or lack thereof, on their behalf.

Even if you get authorities to intervene and the student is taken to a psychiatric hospital for evaluation, their life is still in their hands.

If a student tragically chooses to commit or attempt suicide, you are not responsible for their actions.

You are only responsible for yourself.

If you do have the chance to help a student who is battling the dark thoughts of ending their life, be responsible for yourself in the situation and do everything in your power to come alongside them.

But your role is to do just that—come alongside them.

Unless you are a professional and licensed counselor, therapist, or psychologist, your role as a First Responder is to triage students when they come to you requesting advice or prayer.

What is the definition of *triage*? Here are two definitions from www.dictionary.com to help clarify the term:

1. The process of sorting victims, as a battle of disaster, to determine medical priority in order to increase the number of survivors, and

2. The determination of priorities for action.

When a student comes to you for advice or prayer, they are usually hurting.

It is rare that a student will come to you for advice or prayer because they need help with something good going on in their life. They come to you during difficult times in their lives.

Your role is not to fix them, but to triage them and determine how to get them the best help possible given their specific situation and needs of the moment.

Before you attempt to triage a teenager, be sure to incorporate tip #2.

STEP #2: PROTECT YOURSELF

If you are in a group setting and a student of the opposite sex asks to speak with you, be sure to include another adult leader of the student's same gender for accountability.

In addition, if you see a student of your same gender speaking with a leader of the opposite gender, walk up and gently offer to join the conversation to help the other leader. They may not feel that it's appropriate to leave the conversation to get another leader, so you're being a team player.

While our culture today recognizes dozens of variations of genders, the purpose for positioning yourself with a student of same gender is primarily for your protection rather than the student's.

Remember that teenagers can be very hormonal and impulsive, and each adult leader is one false accusation away from a destroyed reputation.

When a minor makes an accusation against an adult, I have been told the courts side with the minor in 99% of the cases.

While the presumption that you are "innocent until proven guilty" applies to your verdict itself, it may not protect you from being fired from your job, lost relationships, a destroyed reputation, and spending tens of thousands of dollars in lawyer fees.

While you likely work with teenagers for the joy of serving the next generation, it is unwise to risk everything you have for the sake of helping a student who could love you one minute and hate you the next.

Regardless of the gender of the student who comes to you for help, you're already at risk.

What happens if they don't like what you have to say? What if you try to get them the help they need and they perceive your actions as a betrayal of trust?

In your quest to be a Good Samaritan, it could cost you everything if you're not careful.

This is not to suggest that you should be fearful of helping students or that you should resist helping those dealing with anxiety, depression or suicidal thoughts.

I am simply suggesting to help create healthy boundaries in how you communicate with students and with whom you communicate. We do not live in a perfect world, so there are no perfect solutions.

However, if you do your best to come alongside students of the same gender, you are minimizing your risk of false accusations.

While this is not a book to discuss gender definitions or differences, you place yourself in the safest position to help if you try to serve students of your same gender.

If you are unsure of a student's gender or sexuality, this is not the time to assume or ask questions related to the subject—unless, of course, the subject is related to why they are feeling the dark thoughts in the first place.

Do not miss opportunities to help teenagers because you were too concerned about being politically correct. However, do yourself a favor and protect yourself by being above reproach.

STEP #3: DON'T MAKE PROMISES YOU CAN'T KEEP

Students will often initiate a conversation by saying, "If I tell you something, will you promise not to tell anyone else?"

Or, "If I tell you what's going on, will you promise not to tell my parents?"

Because you do not know what they are about to tell you, you cannot make that promise.

You may be tempted to agree to not tell anyone just so you can hear what they want to tell you. However, if they reveal something that needs intervention, you would have to break your word.

There are likely two reasons behind their request for secrecy:

1. They want to feel safe, and
2. They don't want their reputation tarnished

You can still provide safety and protect their reputation if they share with you anyways.

Therefore, let them know that while you can NOT promise you won't tell anyone else, what you CAN promise is that you will help get them the to the right people if what they share requires more assistance than what you can offer.

You MUST tell someone else if the student tells you about any emotional or physical harm that is taking place to himself or herself or to someone they know.

This isn't because you *can't* be trusted—it's because you *can* be trusted. You can be trusted to get them the help they need.

If the student has initiated the conversation, they came to you because they want to get something off their chest. This means they likely will still tell you what they want to share *despite* the fact that you cannot guarantee complete confidentiality.

Be cautious with small groups or Bible studies where leaders will often say things like, "What is said in this group stays in this group."

While your group can and should offer confidentiality for some issues, if a student happens to share something that you are required to share with someone else, you would be forced to break your promise.

> *It is better not to make a vow than to make one and not fulfill it.* –**Ecclesiastes 5:5**

Instead, say something like, "This group is like a family, and this is going to be a safe place. We expect that information shared here will not be used in gossip or shared with others outside this group with whom it should not be shared."

Do not, however, set yourself up for failure by making a blanket promise that you cannot keep down the road.

This isn't to suggest that you have permission to gossip about the student either. In Step #11 I will share when it is appropriate to tell someone else what a student has shared and whom you should tell.

STEP #4: FIND A PLACE TO TALK

This may sound overly basic, but when a student approaches you to talk, you may not be in a physical location where you can actually hear one another.

If you pretend to listen when you can't actually hear what the student is saying, you may inadvertently cause incredible damage by responding poorly out of ignorance.

If the environment around you is loud and it is difficult to hear one another, find a place in a public area where you can hear each other easily.

Do not, however, find an isolated place where nobody is able to see you.

Meet in open areas where anyone can walk by at any time. If you are meeting in an office without a window on the door, keep the door open. Do not meet in dark or shadowy areas when there are lit areas nearby. Do not meet in a parked vehicle with the doors and windows closed.

My point is that you want to avoid the appearance that you are trying to meet in a secretive location.

Again, while your role is to be a First Responder, you also must be diligent to ensure you are protecting yourself and your own reputation.

STEP #5: BE PRESENT

To triage a hurting teenager properly, you need to use your discernment in order to determine what you should do next.

You cannot use your discernment if you are not actively listening to the student.

Be present with the student and listen. Really listen. Here are some pointers for how to actively listen:

- Listen with your face. Listen with your eyes. Silently nod as they speak (if appropriate) to indicate that you're following their story.
- Do not be looking at your phone. Turn your phone on silent. Turn your phone over or put it away.
- Do not be distracted. Do not pay attention to the music playing in the background. Do not acknowledge other students trying to get your attention. Ignore what is happening around you. If distractions around you are too great, you should ask the student if you can find a quieter location to talk. If you do need to find a new location, make sure that it is accessible to the public (See Step #4).

- Do not attempt to multi-task during the conversation. If you are walking from a loud location to a quiet location, do not try to keep up the conversation during your walk. Get to the place where you can focus 100% of your attention on them before resuming your conversation.
- Do not interrupt the student. Wait until they are done talking before you speak.
- Do not be thinking of what to say while they are speaking. Let them finish before you formulate your response, even if it means you are silent for a few seconds in order to gather your thoughts once they have finished speaking.
- Do not try to one-up their story. You might have had a similar situation take place in your life, but if they tell you about something really difficult they're facing, do not say something like, "You think that's bad?! Listen to what happened to me!" This is patronizing and makes them feel like they should not be struggling with their situation. You can show empathy by briefly sharing something similar that you have overcome, but resist the temptation to steer the direction toward your story altogether. Share any empathy you can from personal

experience, but do so briefly only for the purpose of showing you can understand a bit of what they must be feeling, but quickly come back to *their* story, *their* thoughts, and *their* situation.

Failing to listening to a student *well* can inadvertently result in causing more harm than good.

STEP #6: LISTEN FOR WARNING SIGNS

If the student makes any statements similar to the following, consider them warning signs:

- *"I just wish I hadn't been born."*
- *"Nobody would care if I was gone."*
- *"Life isn't worth living anymore."*
- *"I just want to end things."*
- *"My friends wouldn't miss me."*

While the statements above may warrant involvement from someone with more experience, continue to dig deeper rather than running out the door to go get help right away.

The student is unlikely to cause self-harm while they are there with you, and research shows that simply talking about their feelings is a form of therapy.

You likely still need to get additional help, but it won't hurt for you to listen more before you get extra resources.

There are times, however, that you will need to stop your conversation and get help immediately. Such instances include when a student is currently in the process of self-harm or admits to you that they have a plan of action already created for how they will harm or kill themselves.

If you find yourself in an emergency situation as described in the previous paragraph, skip to Step #11 for further instructions.

STEP #7: DON'T FREAK OUT

It is oftentimes the case that students are looking for a reaction from adults.

With pressure to acquire more and more "likes" on social media platforms, it's no wonder why teenagers today are looking for reactions considering they have been trained to crave attention from others.

A student may have just revealed to you information that is causing you to freak out in your mind. However, try to control your reaction despite the fact that what they shared may indeed have shock value.

No matter how crazy the information sounds, freaking out can either cause them to feel unsafe or fuel an unhealthy craving for attention.

This does not mean that you cannot empathize or show grief, but don't seem astonished or shocked at what they say.

Be aware that your resting face has the ability to freak out for you even if your words don't. Therefore, try to control what you communicate non-verbally by attempting to not show astonishment or shock in your face or body language.

STEP #8: KEEP ASKING QUESTIONS

Even if the student shares some of the warning signs listed from Step #6—while you do likely need to get them additional help—continue to ask the student open-ended questions.

Oftentimes their act of sharing what is on their mind and being heard is an effective form of therapy on its own.

If the student has opened up about suicidal feelings within the context of a small group, do not ask further questions about it with other students around.

Simply say something like, "I'd like to ask you more about that after our group." You do not want to have a serious conversation about suicide with a suicidal student in the presence of other students.

On the other hand, you do not want to dismiss their statement altogether if they said something in front of others.

By ignoring their comment—even if you have the intention to follow up with them later privately—you communicate to other students around you that you are dismissive with such dire statements.

By acknowledging it publicly and discussing it privately with the student as soon as possible without other students around, you are communicating to the group that you can be trusted to follow up with teenagers without embarrassing or ignoring them.

Once you are in a safe and protected place to chat with your student, some good open-ended questions to ask are:

- *"Tell me more about what you mentioned earlier."*
- *"Why are you feeling the way you do?"*
- *"Did something recently happen that made you feel that way?"*
- *"When did you start feeling this way?"*
- *"Do you feel like this a lot?"*

As they answer your questions, you will gain more information to help you determine how to best triage.

If you feel the student may be suicidal, do not shy away from the question you are wondering.

According to the National Suicide Hotline, you should go ahead and pose the question on your mind by directly asking:

- *"Are you suicidal?"*

Don't be afraid to ask bluntly. You need to be forthright with the question if you are genuinely concerned. Typically students will be honest with how they respond.

If they say "no", you may be able to handle the situation with biblical advice, prayer, and presenting a few options for what they can do next.

If they say "yes" to your suicidal question, ask some follow-up questions:

- *"Have you ever attempted suicide in the past?"*
- *"If so, how many times?"*
- *"When was the last time you attempted suicide?"*
- *"How did you try and what happened?"*

If they have mentioned suicide in your conversation or admitted to being suicidal, it is crucial to ask them:

- *"Do you have a plan?"*

For someone who is suicidal, this is the most important question you can ask.

Teens can be very impulsive, and if they already have created a plan for suicide, they need professional help immediately.

If they admit to you that they have a plan, make it your first priority to get them immediate professional assistance.

Do not, however, leave the teenager alone if they are currently suicidal. Call or text someone else to come and help you if necessary.

In addition, you want to keep the teen talking. In most situations, the extreme desire to end one's life will dissipate within about 45 minutes. If you can keep the teen talking for 45 minutes, their desire to end their life may have diminished greatly while they have been talking with you.

If you are not physically present with the person, keep them engaged in conversation on the phone or via texting.

You may also ask them to give you their word that they won't harm themselves for the rest of the day. Even though they may be considering ending their life, they are still likely to care about honoring their word and will be less likely to harm themselves if they have promised you they won't.

For suggestions for who to call if the teenager has admitted that they have already created a plan for suicide, skip to Step #11.

STEP #9: REASSURE THEM

Teenagers want to know they aren't alone, so remind them of what may seem obvious to you, but may not be apparent to them.

Simply say: *"You aren't alone."*

No matter what they just told you, thank them for sharing with you.

Let them know it takes courage to speak up and be vulnerable.

Let them know they aren't in this by themselves, and that you will do what you can to help them in this journey.

However, don't give them this reassurance if you don't mean it. If you tell them they aren't alone and then you take off and leave with no follow up, you have likely worsened their situation by causing them to be reluctant to trust the next person who seems willing to help.

You must be ready to walk this journey with them—at least to the point where you have helped get them to someone who can assist them more than you can.

STEP #10: GIVE SOLID ADVICE

Sharing your opinion can be dangerous if you are not confident the advice you're sharing is actually good advice.

My suggestion is to make sure that anything you share is something you can back up from the Bible. There is no greater authority of Truth, so if you are unsure about what the Bible says about the subject, DO NOT OFFER ADVICE.

This is of utmost importance. Instead, just be honest and say that you aren't sure of the right thing to do, but you will help them find it.

One of the biggest mistakes you can make as a leader is to share advice with good intentions, but inadvertently give bad or unbiblical advice.

If in doubt, err on the side of not sharing in that moment until you know what you're sharing is actually good advice.

If you ever discover that you gave poor or unbiblical advice to someone in the past, be sure to circle back with that student and let them know of your mistake and correct the advice you gave.

STEP #11: TRIAGE THEM

This is the time when you help determine their next steps and the order in which they should take them.

Based on all the information you have acquired in your conversation, you have only 2 directions you can go:

1. Handle it yourself.

Although they likely came to you to share what's on their mind, don't automatically assume they want to hear your advice.

If you believe your advice for their situation is what they currently need, get permission to share your thoughts before you share them. Ask them something like:

- *"Can I make a suggestion for what you could try?"*
- *"Would you like some advice?"*
- *"I have some thoughts. Would you like to hear them?"*

Once they give you permission to share, be sure to share solid advice. To ensure you're sharing good advice, see Step #10.

The only other triage option you have is to invite someone else to the conversation who can help the teenager more than you can. Therefore, your only other option is this:

2. Invite one more person to the conversation.

While you only have two directions you can take in your triage, part of this second direction is determining *whom* you need to invite to the conversation.

Remember, part of your role as a First Responder is to help them feel safe and protected. You are not in the position to take what they have shared and tell other students or leaders.

Below is a list of people you can invite to the conversation, in the order in which you should invite them. If one person is not available, move to the next down the list.

- Youth Pastor / Minister
- Parent

- Professional Counselor
- Police

In some situations, you may need to bypass some of the recommended people and contact the National Suicide Hotline or police. Use your discretion.

Let's clarify each of the people on the list mentioned on the previous page.

- Youth Pastor / Minister

If you are a volunteer at a church, contact the Youth Pastor immediately, even if it is after regular working hours. If the church does not have a Youth Pastor, contact any Pastor or Minister on staff.

The Youth Pastor may have additional information about the student, possibly including previous interactions related to the same situation.

If the Youth Pastor is busy or unavailable and the situation is *not* an emergency, then you may be able to wait until you can speak directly with the Youth Pastor depending on your circumstances. If you are in doubt about whether you should include someone else in the conversation right away, it is better to assume that you should rather than opting to wait.

If the Youth Pastor is unavailable and you need an additional person to be brought into the conversation immediately, then contact the teenager's parents.

- Parent

If the student shares with you that a parent is part of the problem (such as abuse), then contacting the parent may not be the best option. Use your discernment.

The parent likely has more insight into the situation than you know, and may have already taken steps to help alleviate the situation.

If you need to contact a parent, give the student 4 options:

1. The student can call the parent and tell them what is on their mind. Then you can speak to the parent while they are still on the phone to verify what the student shared with them is the same as what the student shared with you.

2. The student can call the parent on speakerphone with you in the room. This provides the accountability knowing that what they told you is what is also said to the parent.
3. You can call the parent on the student's behalf. This would typically be with the student in the room while you call their parent on speakerphone.
4. You can wait to speak with the parent if they are picking up their teenager once you are done with your conversation.

While you are giving the student options for how to contact the parent, do not give the student an option that does not include contacting the parent, unless you have reason to believe contacting the parent could cause more harm.

A third option for who to include in the conversation is:

- Counselor

Depending on your physical location with relation to the student, you have a few options to connect a teenager with a counselor qualified to talk with people who are suicidal.

If you are physically present with the student, call the National Suicide Hotline at 800-273-8255 while on speakerphone. The line is open and trained counselors are available 24/7. They will assist with your triage and help determine next steps for the student for you. You can also text the hotline if the student is not comfortable calling for whatever reason.

If the student contacts you from school, encourage them to go see their school counselor immediately. If they are worried about missing an assignment or test, they can make it up if they are in the counselor's office. This situation is of greater importance than any classes or tests they may be missing. If a student is unwilling to go see the counselor, then call the school yourself and ask to speak with the counselor regarding a suicidal student.

If the student contacts you and you don't know where they are, let them know they have options for professional counselors. See the list of counselors in the Quick Reference Guide on page 54 to make suggestions for who they can call. You can also offer to create a group text with the National Suicide Hotline so you can know they are getting help in real time.

A fourth option for who to include in your conversation is your local police department.

- Police

If a student is threatening to harm him or herself, is currently harming him or herself, or admits they have a plan for suicide and the student is with you or you know where the student is located, contact the police immediately.

If you believe the teen may flee if you contact the police, you can also try texting 911. Most 911 switchboards are now set up to receive text messages.

Here are a few tips for calling the police:
- Do not call the non-emergency line. This situation warrants an emergency. Call or text 911.
- Ask the 911 operator for the psychiatric suicidal unit. Nearly every police force has officers trained to deal with people who are suicidal. They will attempt to send you officers specifically trained for your situation.

Be aware that if you do call the police, the situation will no longer be in your hands. The officers who arrive on the scene may or may not listen to your suggestions, and may make choices with which you do not agree. That is okay.

You are following a series of steps, and by making the choice to include the police, you are ensuring the best care available to you in the moment.

It is better for you to err on the side of precaution than to let a teenager leave your presence who just admitted to having suicidal thoughts.

In most situations, police officers will attempt to contact parents or will contact paramedics depending on the severity of the situation.

If the police contact paramedics, the paramedics will likely also err on the side of caution since they are not trained counselors or psychologists.

This means they will take the teenager via ambulance to a hospital for admittance. If this occurs, the teenager will have no choice in the matter and may be restrained by the paramedics and/or police if they try to resist.

Once the teenager arrives to the hospital, they will be scheduled to undergo a psychological evaluation as soon as possible.

Such evals are typically conducted during regular working hours, so if the teenager arrives to the hospital after hours, they will likely be required to spend the night while they are placed under suicide watch.

An average hospital stay for a suicidal patient can range from 12-72 hours.

While an ambulance trip and a hospital stay can be a very expensive proposition, if you have exhausted your other options other than contacting the police, you have no choice but to include authorities.

It is worth mentioning that the National Suicide Hotline can be utilized by non-suicidal people as well.

If you are in a situation and are unsure of your next best move, feel free to contact the hotline yourself so they can help reassure you of what to do next.

Every person who answers the hotline is a trained professional and certified to deal with people who are suicidal.

STEP #12: EQUIP THEM

Depending on what the teenager needs, be sure to equip them before they leave your presence.

Below is a list of resources you can provide directly to the teenager.

EMERGENCIES

Police: 911 (call or text)
National Suicide Hotline: 800-273-8255 (call or text)

NON-EMERGENCIES (all accept low to no income patients)

WARM LINE: For people who need extra support before being in an actual crisis. A "hotline" is for those who are in immediate danger whereas a "warm line" is created for those who are not in immediate danger.
800-930-9276

WALK-IN CLINICS: Connects at-risk people to professional counselors. Do a Google search for "walk-in counselor clinics" in your area.

CRISIS HOUSES: For people who consider themselves safe, but feel like they need to check in somewhere so they don't take harmful action. Crisis Houses include accountability, medication management, and group therapy. They may require a referral, but patients can often refer themselves.

CLUB HOUSES: Connect at-risk people with others going through the similar situations or experiencing similar thoughts.

STEP #13: FOLLOW UP

Help the teen actually take the next step you suggested. If you believe they may not take the step, have them take the next step while they are with you.

Regardless of whether the situation was serious enough to involve another person, set an alarm to call or text them the next day to check in.

Do not wait a full week or until you happen to see them again before following up.

QUICK REFERENCE GUIDE

EMERGENCIES

Police: 911 (call or text)

National Suicide Hotline: 800-273-8255 (call or text)

NON-EMERGENCIES (all accept low to no income patients)

WARM LINE: For people who need extra support before being in a crisis. A "hotline" is for those who are in immediate danger whereas a "warm line" is created for those who are not in immediate danger.
800-930-9276

WALK-IN CLINICS: Connects at-risk people to professional counselors. Do a Google search for "walk-in counselor clinics" in your area.

CRISIS HOUSES: For people who consider themselves safe, but feel like they need to check in somewhere so they don't take action. Crisis Houses include accountability, medication management, and group therapy. They may require a referral, but patients can often refer themselves.

CLUB HOUSES: Connect at-risk people with others going through the similar situations or experiencing similar thoughts.

CONCLUSION

Don't assume that what a teen shares with you is "no big deal".

If someone tells you they are considering ending their life, do your best to come alongside that person to get them the help they need, whether they want it or not.

While ultimately you are not responsible for their actions, they may be thankful down the road that you took the time to help them when they seemed to be in a fog.

Best of luck as you navigate each difficult conversation.

I'm praying for you in advance.

ACKNOWLEDGEMENTS

A special thanks to each organization and person who helped with the ideas, thoughts, editing, publication, and distribution of this book, including the National Suicide Hotline, Suicide Prevention Resource Center, The Jason Foundation, and:

Ashten Mizell
Aseneth Murphy
Daren DeShon
Kathy Kirk
Keenan Klamer
Kindra French
Liane Davis
Linsey Welton
Lorie Phillips
Monica DeShon
Rebekah Dahlquist
Steven Murphy
Tim Dahlquist
Tom Skawski

ABOUT THE AUTHOR

Matt has worked with teenagers for over two decades. Prior to the release of Netflix's series "Thirteen Reasons Why", Matt experienced a night in youth ministry when 3 students admitted they were contemplating suicide with one attempt at the church while students were on campus.

As he was driving home after midnight having triaged all 3 students that he realized that he couldn't be the sole person available in times of crisis when he clearly could not be in multiple places at the same time.

As a result, Matt contacted counselors, therapists, and even called the National Suicide Hotline to put together a resource that could be used by his own volunteer leaders if they are ever find themselves in a conversation with a suicidal teenager.

Get to know Matt at www.mattmizell.com.

Get Matt's 3-week sermon series titled

Thirteen Reasons Why NOT

to teach students how to handle anxiety, depression, and suicidal thoughts in a healthy and biblical way.

Download the series for free today at www.mattmizell.com/13-reasons-why-not-series.

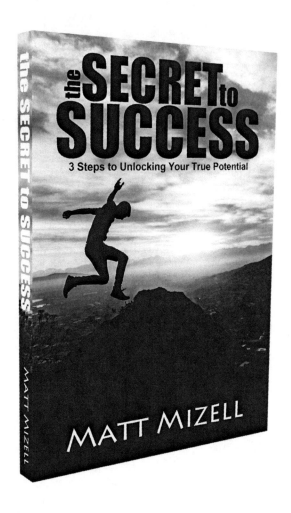

Learn how to be successful in God's eyes by downloading a free copy of Matt's book,

The Secret to Success

3 Steps to Unlocking Your True Potential,
by visiting www.mattmizell.com/success.

Create buzz & excitement for your brand using cutting-edge advertising by downloading a free copy of Matt's book,

The Complete Guide to Building Your Brand With Snapchat

by visiting www.mattmizell.com/snapchat.

Add Matt as a friend on Snapchat using the Snapcode above. To do so, open the Snapchat camera and tap and hold the screen on the Snapcode above. Your device should automatically find Matt's profile to add him as a friend.

Learn how to build a legacy and become a better leader by joining the movement at www.mattmizell.com.

#leaderworthfollowing

CPSIA information can be obtained
at www.ICGtesting.com
Printed in the USA
LVOW07s0626170517
534803LV00008B/180/P